Table of Contents

Chapter 1: Basic Economics Concepts

Chapter 2: Financial Literacy Concepts

Chapter 3: Business Concepts

Chapter 1 Project

Make a graphic organizer summarizing a few key ideas for each of these following terms:

- Community
- Complements
- Free Enterprise
- Goods
- Services
- Philanthropy
- Profit
- Nonprofit
- Economy
- Scarcity
- Substitutes
- Supply
- Demand
- Market Economy
- Opportunity Cost

Chapter 1 Basic Economic Concepts

CHAPTER 1:

Basic Economics Concepts

Hello! My name is Orpple. I am very excited right now, because I am contributing to a bake sale fundraiser by baking banana nut muffins - my favorite! I might sneak a bite here and there, but I promise that the majority of the muffins will make their way to the fundraiser. At least, let's hope so.

Looking around my kitchen, I don't have all the ingredients necessary to make banana nut muffins! I guess I have to go to my local store. Let's go; I'll bring you along with me!

Hey Orpple! I'm cleaning up our neighborhood by picking up trash.

Hi, Mr. Steve, Ora, and Bana!

Wow, what a great community of people this is!

COMMUNITY

A **community** is a group of people who live in the same area or who have a common interest. For example, your community could include your neighborhood, classmates, and teachers. If you are a dancer, you can refer to the large group of dancers as your dance community.

 VERSUS

Okay, so I only need to go to one store, but I have two choices. Which one should I go to? Both FoodLand and AllFoods have similar foods and prices, which means that they're competing businesses. After all, this is a market economy that follows the free enterprise system.

MARKET ECONOMY

A market is a place where people can exchange goods and services. Your local grocery store, a local factory, and a local recreation center are all examples of markets. At a grocery store, food is exchanged for money. At a local factory, workers exchange their labor for wages. At a recreation center, money is exchanged for leisure. Markets are everywhere in our daily lives! In a **market economy**, goods and services are privately owned and a profit incentive exists.

Chapter 1 Basic Economic Concepts

FREE ENTERPRISE SYSTEM

You have the freedom to buy a house, eat cookies, and choose what color to paint your room. You have the freedom to decide what to do, and what not to do, without excessive government control over your actions. Essentially, you have the right to make decisions for yourself. The basis of the **free enterprise system** is supply and demand.

> I decided to go to FoodLand, because who doesn't want to visit a land full of food? Looking around, I can tell that FoodLand offers many goods and services.

GOODS & SERVICES

Goods are physical items that satisfy the wants of buyers. Banana tarts, bagels, textbooks, and laptops are all examples of goods because they can be touched or held. Everyone consumes goods in their daily lives! Unsurprisingly, these goods are also known as consumer goods.

Services are intangible actions that satisfy the wants of buyers. Services are activities such as providing haircuts, medical examinations, dining services, and education to the consumers.

All buying actions involve either a good or a service!

Okay, friends! Let's look at the banana nut muffin recipe and see what I need to buy. First of all, I need butter!

But...uh oh... the store doesn't have any butter left! It looks like I'm not the only one wanting to make muffins. I will have to substitute coconut oil for butter, since it looks like the store only has coconut oil.

Chapter 1 Basic Economic Concepts

SUBSTITUTES & COMPLEMENTS

Substitutes are goods that could be used instead of another good. Substitute goods are important in economics because they greatly influence consumer choices. In the market, when the price of one good increases, consumers can purchase a substitute good. For example, if the price of butter increases, consumers can purchase coconut oil instead because they are substitutes. Substitute goods can easily be replaced with each other.

Complements are goods that are used together. For example, muffins and milk, coffee and cream, and hotdogs and hotdog buns.

Now, I have everything I need to make my muffins! I am back at home, and it's time to start baking! I have a small problem: I really want to make 100 muffins, but I, unfortunately, cannot. This is because of scarcity.

SCARCITY

All valued resources are limited, meaning they are **scarce**! For example, think of the lined paper in your binder. Once you use them all, you will not have any paper left. This means that lined paper is a limited resource and is scarce. Additionally, on farms, trees are cut down to make paper. If too many trees are cut down, then there would not be enough trees to produce paper. Therefore, trees are another example of a limited resource.

I wish that the trees around me were unlimited! Sadly, that's not the case.

Now that you have learned about the idea of scarcity and limited resources, you understand why we have to make choices. Our wants are unlimited, but resources are limited. This means that we cannot have everything we want, and we have to make choices.

I baked my muffins! I only had enough resources to make 50 muffins. By the way, I am a good monkey and only ate 5 so far.

Chapter 1 Basic Economic Concepts

> I arrived at the fundraiser! The fundraiser is hosted by a nonprofit organization.

NONPROFIT & PROFIT

A **nonprofit** is an organization that works to serve people, rather than to make money. While nonprofits can earn money, the money goes back to employees and other areas that help the nonprofit carry out its mission. Nonprofits that pass certain government standards can receive 501(c)(3), tax-exempt status. 501(c)(3) organizations don't have to pay taxes on the money they earn because all of their money is being used to serve the public.

Profit is the money that a for-profit business makes. Profit = total revenue - total expenses. Businesses exist to make profits from the goods or services that they sell. For example, if a clothing store sells t-shirts for 20 dollars each when it only costs them 5 dollars to produce a shirt, then their profit for each t-shirt sold would be $20 - $5 = $15 profit.

> Wow, there are a lot of people at the fundraiser! The attendees demand the baked goods while the contributors (including me) supply them!

Chapter 1 Basic Economic Concepts

SUPPLY & DEMAND

Buyers are the consumers of goods and services; thus, they create **demand**. Demand is created when a consumer is able and willing to buy a certain good at a set price, assuming all other factors are held constant. Let's say that you are at the mall with your parents. If you are financially able to buy a pair of jeans and you want that pair of jeans, then you are creating demand! However, even if you really want those jeans, but are not able to afford them, you are not actually demanding that good. So, when people buy a good or service, they are both able and willing to purchase it!

The other side of the market is **supply**. Supply is the amount of a good or service that producers are willing and able to sell at set prices. When you go shopping, all of the goods on the shelves of stores are supplied by the store!

Demand and supply come together to create the basis of the market system. Buyers demand goods and services, and suppliers supply goods and services to meet the demands of the buyers! See how everything is coming together?

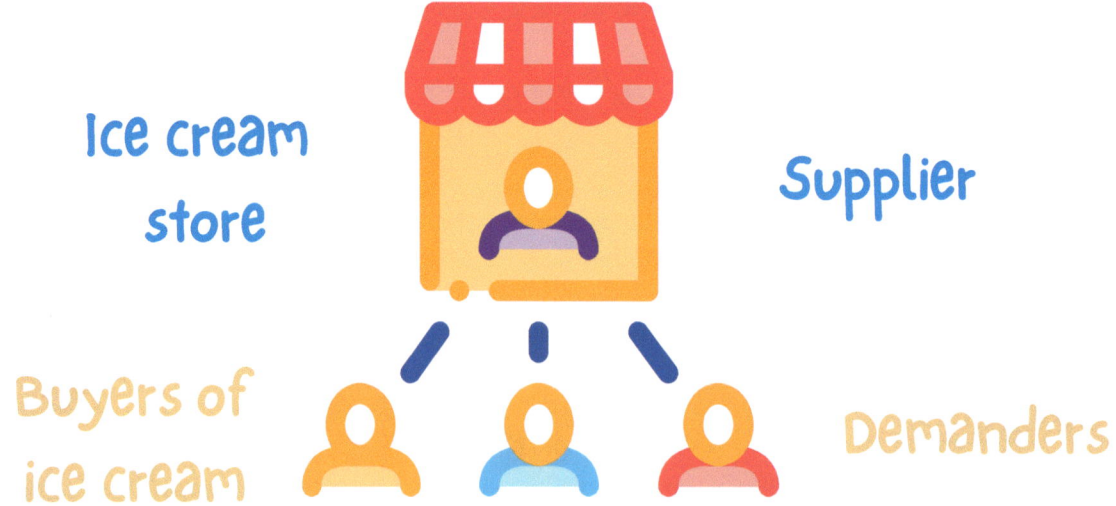

11   Chapter 1 Basic Economic Concepts

It feels so good to be fundraising for a charitable cause. After all, it's an act of philanthropy!

PHILANTHROPY

Philanthropy is the desire to help others in order to create a better society. It is carried out by donating money, time, or goods to charities or organizations. Donating money to a nonprofit, volunteering for a charity, and donating toys to a toy drive are all examples of philanthropy.

I arrived back home! Oh my goodness, I spent 5 hours baking these muffins and attending the fundraiser! At least my opportunity cost was low, because I finished all of my homework before the fundraiser.

     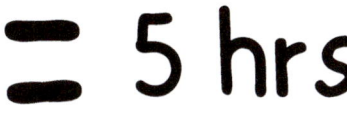

OPPORTUNITY COST

Opportunity cost is the value lost from the second best thing that could have been chosen (but was not chosen). For example, pretend that Orpple has two choices for a task to complete in the next hour:

        1.) Watch a movie
        2.) Practice piano.

If Orpple chooses to watch a movie, he would not be able to practice piano. Therefore, Orpple's opportunity cost of watching a movie would be the value of practicing piano for an hour.

 V.S.

> Friends, my journey today displays many key economic concepts! Our economy is awesome!

ECONOMY

An **economy** is a system of producing and selling goods and services of value. An economy involves sellers (producers) and buyers (consumers) who exchange money for goods and services or time for payment. An economy also includes trade with foreign countries.

What is Economics?

Now that you've dipped your toes into the world of economics... what exactly is it?

ECONOMICS

is the study of

SCARCITY  and

CHOICE

Chapter 1 Basic Economic Concepts

Diving a little Deeper...

Let's have some fun!!!

Instructions: there will be a series of questions on key economic concepts learned in this chapter. Simply think about (or write down) the corresponding answer choices and check to see if you are correct on the next page!

1. **True or False:** A nonprofit organization has a primary motivation of making money.

2. In a market economy:
   a. All goods and services are owned by the government
   b. there is a profit incentive
   c. There is no competition

3. Are banana tarts goods or services?
   a. Goods
   b. Services

4. Is the action of a chef baking a banana tart a good or a service?
   a. Good
   b. Service

5. Is the person who is selling a water bottle a supplier or a demander?
   a. Supplier
   b. Demander

6. **True or False:** A market is where children grades K-5 go to play (slides, swings, etc.).

7. Are fries and ketchup substitutes or complements?
   a. Substitutes
   b. Complements

8. **True or False:** all resources are unlimited.

9. What is a philanthropist?
   a. Someone who works to make a profit.
   b. Someone who donates money
   c. A race car driver
   d. Someone who buys books from a used book store

10. **True or False:** In a free enterprise system, people have the freedom to own property and make decisions for themselves.

ANSWER KEY

1. False; a nonprofit organization has a primary motivation of serving people rather than making money.

2. B; in a market economy, goods and services are owned by individual companies and companies compete with each other for the purpose of making money (earning profit).

3. Goods; banana tarts are physical items that can be touched and held.

4. Service; the action of the chef baking the banana tart satisfies the wants of buyers.

5. Supplier; a seller of a good or service is the supplier of the good or service. the demander, on the other hand, is the buyer who purchases the good or service supplied by the supplier (seller).

6. False; a market is where goods and services are exchanged.

7. Complements; fries and ketchup are often used together, and therefore are complements. Fries and ketchup are not substitutes (goods that can be used in place of one another), because you wouldn't eat ketchup in place of fries, or dip fries in fries (it doesn't make sense!).

8. False; all resources are limited! Although people have unlimited wants (unlimited paper, food, pens, etc.), the unlimited wants can never be satisfied due to limited resources.

9. Philanthropy is the act of helping other people or donating. A philanthropist is someone who aspires to promote the well-being of others, often donating money to needy people or to a certain cause.

10. True; In the free enterprise system, people have the right to own property and make decisions for themselves.

Chapter 2 Project

Make a foldable that details the following terms (pictures can be included):

- Account Number
- Deposit Ticket
- Checkbook Register
- Endorse Signature
- Checking Account
- Loan
- Checks
- Net Deposit
- Deposit
- Savings Account

CHAPTER 2: Financial Literacy Concepts

Yay! We raised over $500 dollars from the large bake sale fundraiser for a nonprofit. Now, we need to deposit the money into the nonprofit's bank account. I'm in charge of that! Come with me!

DEPOSIT & DEPOSIT TICKET

A **deposit** occurs when someone puts a certain amount of money into a bank account. People deposit money into their bank accounts when they get paid or would like to keep their money safe. Many monetary deposits into bank accounts can be taken out easily when the person needs to spend the money.

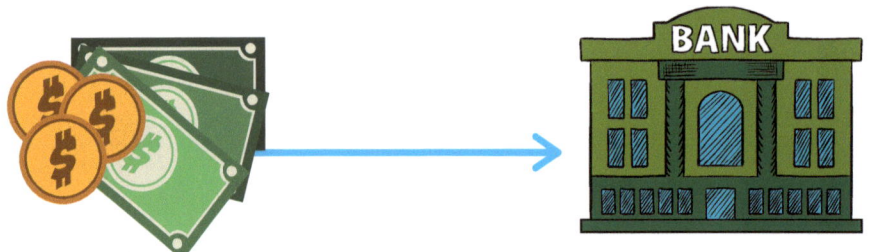

A **deposit ticket** is a receipt that a depositor (the person who puts money into the bank) receives when money is deposited. A deposit ticket includes the following information: date, name, bank account number, signature, cash, checks, cash withdrawal, and the total (net deposit).

Chapter 2 Financial Literacy Concepts

The nonprofit we fundraised for has a checking account, so we'll see how that works!

CHECKING & SAVINGS ACCOUNTS

A **checking account** is a type of bank account that is used for daily transactions (spending money and putting money into the bank account). With a checking account, the account holder can take money out of their bank account by writing checks.

A **savings account** is a type of bank account that allows the depositing and removing of money while the money in the bank account earns interest. Interest is the additional money earned by the owner of the bank account (paid by the bank) from depositing a certain amount of money into the bank account.

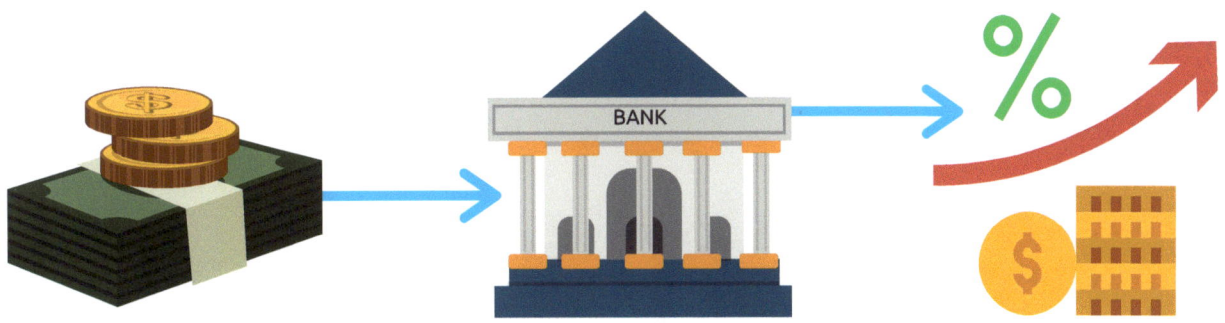

> I have written a check of $500, which will be deposited into the nonprofit's bank account. The check has my endorsed signature on it.

CHECKS

Checks are written slips that tell a bank to pay for something from your bank account. A check includes information such as an address, date, the name of the person or organization that will receive the money, the amount of money written in words, the amount of money written in numbers, and a memo line for additional information.

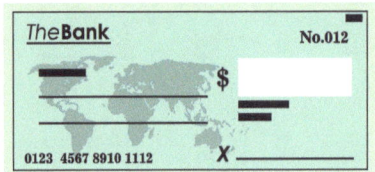 

ENDORSE SIGNATURE

An **endorse signature** is the signature at the back of a check, signed by the person paying the amount of money as said on the check. This signature proves that the payer of the money intend the money to the person specified on the check.

21 Chapter 2 Financial Literacy Concepts

In order to deposit the check, I need the account number. I'm going to ask the nonprofit's treasurer for the number!

ACCOUNT NUMBER

Every bank account owner has a unique **account number**, which is a number that associates an owner with the bank account and allows the account's owner to access the bank account. Account numbers enhance the security and privacy of a bank account.

Since the nonprofit had previously taken out a loan, hopefully our money can cover it!

LOAN

A **loan** is an amount of money that is lent to a certain person or organization under an agreement that the money will be paid back in the future.

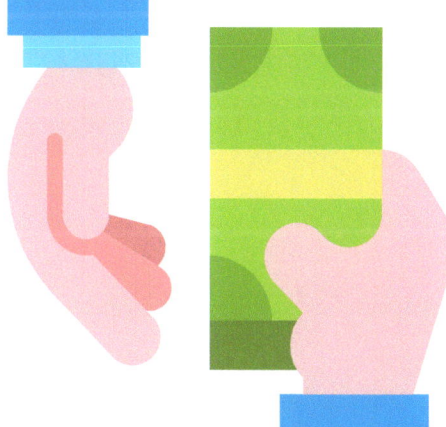

Now that I deposited the money, I need to update the nonprofit's checkbook register.

CHECKBOOK REGISTER

A **checkbook register** is a document that helps a person or an organization keep track of all financial transactions and their account balance. A checkbook register includes the following information: check number, date, transaction description, payment/debit, deposit/debit, and balance.

> Wow! The money did cover the loan. Now the nonprofit's net deposit is a positive number.

NET DEPOSIT

The **net deposit** is known as the total deposits (money put into the bank account) minus the total withdrawals (money taken out of the bank account) that were made using a certain method of payment. If the total deposits are greater than the total withdrawals, then the net deposit would be positive; if the total deposits are less than the total withdrawals, then the net deposit would be negative.

> Friends, my depositing of the money fundraised shows some important financial concepts! Now, you've traveled into the word of finance!

Diving a little Deeper...

Let's have some fun!!!

Instructions: there will be a series of questions on key financial literacy concepts learned in this chapter. Simply think about (or write down) the corresponding answer choices and check to see if you are correct on the next page!

• •

1. **True or False:** A deposit ticket is a receipt provided when someone deposits money into his or her bank account.

2. I don't have enough money. I should apply for a...
    a. Loan
    b. Check

3. **True or False:** All bank account owners have the same account numbers.

4. I want a _____ for my everyday spending and saving.
    a. Savings account
    b. Checking account

5. **True or False:** A checking account and a savings account serve the same purpose.

6. **True or False:** A check can be used to buy a t-shirt at a school event.

7. I want to keep track of my spending and saving. I should use a...
    a. Check
    b. Checkbook Register

8. If I had a total deposit of $500 and had a total withdrawal of $100, my net deposit would be...
    a. Positive
    b. Negative

9. **True or False:** A deposit ticket is a type of deposit.

10. Endorse signatures are used to...
    a. Serve as decoration on the check.
    b. Show that the payer has a purpose of paying the specified amount of money on the check to the receiver

Chapter 2 Financial Literacy Concepts

ANSWER KEY

1. True; deposit tickets are receipts that are given to the depositor with the necessary information.

2. A; if someone doesn't have enough money, they would apply for a loan, since the person would be borrowing a certain amount of money to use for now and would pay it back later.

3. False; all bank account owners have different, unique account numbers in order to correctly identify the owner of a certain bank account.

4. Checking account; checking accounts are used for everyday transactions.

5. False; A checking account and a savings account serve different purposes. A checking account is used for daily transactions while a savings account is used for putting money away (saving) for future use.

6. True; checks can be used in place of cash to transfer an amount of money to another person or organization as a payment.

7. Checkbook Register; a checkbook register is a chart used to organize the amount of money that leaves and enters a bank account.

8. A; the net deposit would be positive, because the total deposit is greater than the total withdrawal. This means that more money was put into the bank account than was taken out.

9. False; a deposit ticket is a document stating that a deposit has been made. A deposit is the money that enters a bank account.

10. B; endorse signatures are found on checks to ensure that the owner of the bank account wants to pay a certain amount of money to the person specified on the check.

Chapter 3 Project

Make a poster explaining the following terms:

Advertise	Business Costs	Career
Management	Merchandise	Operating Costs
Readiness	Receipt	Revenue
Sell	Skill	Promissory Note

Chapter 3 Basic Business Concepts

CHAPTER 3:

Business Concepts

I've discovered a real passion for baking banana nut muffins. Wow. From what I've heard (and from what I've tasted), my muffins taste really good. I've been considering this for a while now... should I start a banana nut muffin business? What do you think? Let's think about it. I definitely have a skill for baking banana nut muffins.

SKILL

A **skill** is the ability to do something well. For example, bakery workers are skilled at making cakes. Construction workers are skilled at building bridges.

> I can totally see myself with a career as a chef. I believe my readiness level is very high, and I have great management skills.

CAREER

A **career** is a job someone holds for a significant period of time. People get paid wages or salaries for working.

READINESS

Readiness is how prepared someone is for a certain job. For example, a fifth grader is ready to go to middle school. A professional pianist is ready to give a piano concert.

MANAGEMENT

Management is the practice of supervising a project or people. For instance, the president of an organization is in charge of managing a group of employees.

You know what, why not? I'm going to start a banana nut muffin business. The muffins would be my merchandise.

MERCHANDISE

Merchandise are goods that can be bought by consumers and sold by producers. Other examples of merchandise include books at the book fair, planners from an online store, and laptops from a technology company.

 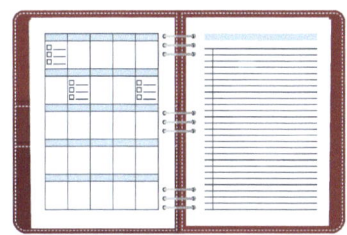 

I filled out the necessary forms to file my business! First, I need money to buy things such as muffin tin liners, more baking trays (I only have one right now), and a new oven. To get the money, my business is going to issue a promissory note.

PROMISSORY NOTE

A **promissory note** is a paper that is signed by someone promising to pay a certain amount of money to another person or organization at the specified date or time.

> Yay, I'm so excited! I hope I will sell many muffins through my business and earn revenue.

SELL & REVENUE

Selling is the act of giving something away in exchange for payment. For example, the pizza shop sells you pizza! You get pizza if you pay for it.

Revenue is the income that a business receives from selling their goods or services. Revenue is calculated by multiplying price by the quantity of goods sold. For example, if an apple store sells 25 apples at 4 dollars each, then their revenue would be 25 x 4 = $100. Revenue = price x quantity sold.

> In order to earn money, I need to advertise my product: banana nut muffins!

ADVERTISE

Advertising is the act of grabbing the attention of potential buyers in hope of selling a product or service or increasing the audience size at an event. For example, a coffee shop would advertise their coffee in order to attract more customers, which would increase the shop's revenue.

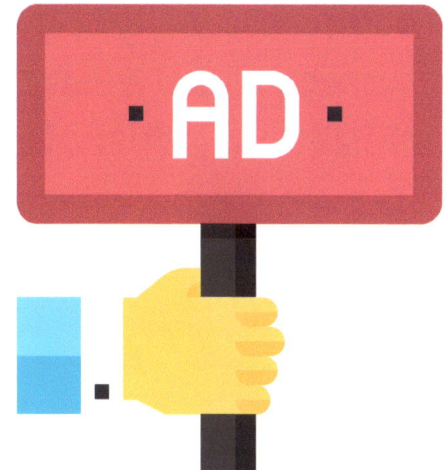

> Okay. I have a very important decision to make now. How should I price my banana nut muffins? $0.50 per muffin? $1 per muffin? To make a proper pricing decision, I have to consider my business costs and my operating costs. One example of something I would have to pay for is receipt paper.

BUSINESS & OPERATING COSTS

Business costs are the costs that a business encounters while it is operating. For instance, payments given to workers would be business costs.

Operating costs are the costs that a business encounters on a daily basis. An example of an operating cost is the money needed to advertise the business's good or service.

RECEIPT

A **receipt** is a written document that confirms a transaction between two people or organizations. Whenever you buy something from a store, you will get a receipt stating what you bought and how much you paid for the goods or services.

Wow, you've been along this whole journey with me! From the fundraiser, to putting in the check, to starting my business, you've accompanied me. I hope you learned a lot!

Diving a little Deeper...

Let's have some fun!!!

Instructions: there will be a series of questions on key business concepts learned in this chapter. Simply think about (or write down) the corresponding answer choices and check to see if you are correct on the next page!

1. **True or False:** If someone is a brilliant violin player, then he or she is an advertisement.

2. **Fill in the blank:** A writer is _____ at writing articles.
   a. Managed
   b. Skilled

3. Someone's _____ is what they do for a living.
   a. Revenue
   b. Career

4. Once a product is bought, a _____ is usually given to the customer.
   a. Promissory note
   b. Receipt

5. If a student graduated from medical school, then he or she is _____ to be a doctor.
   a. Operating
   b. Ready

6. **True or False:** A business advertises its product to show the product's weak points.

7. Betty Apple Shop sold 6 apples at 2 dollars each. What is Betty Apple Shop's revenue?
   a. $8.   c. $12
   b. $15   d. $4

8. **Fill in the blank:** Betty Apple Shop _____ apples.
   a. Consumes
   b. Sells

9. **Fill in the blank:** The CEO of Betty Apple Shop is part of the _____ that oversees its employees.
   a. Management
   b. Merchandise

10. **Fill in the blank:** Betty Apple Shop's _____ includes candied apple and apple ornaments.
    a. Career
    b. Merchandise

ANSWER KEY

1. False; a skill is something that someone is good at. Therefore, if someone is good at violin, then playing violin is a skill they have.

2. B; writers are good at writing, which means that writing is one of their skills.

3. B; a career is someone's job, which is something they do for a living.

4. B; after a good or service is bought by the buyer, a receipt is given to him or her to verify the purchase.

5. B; going to medical school prepares the student for becoming a doctor, so he or she is ready to be a doctor after graduation.

6. False; a business advertises its product to try to sell more of it, so they try to show the product's strong points.

7. C; revenue = price × quantity. In this case, the price of each apple is $2 and the quantity sold is 6 apples. Revenue = 2 × 6 = $12.

8. B; shops sell goods for consumers to purchase.

9. A; management is the process of supervising people. At Betty Apple Shop, the CEO is part of the group of people who control the employees.

10. B; merchandise refers to the goods being sold at a store.

GLOSSARY

Account number
The unique number that connects an owner with a bank account.

Advertise
The act of grabbing the attention of potential buyers in an effort to sell a product or service.

Business Costs
The costs that a business needs to pay in order to operate.

Career
A job someone holds for a significant period of time.

Checkbook register
A document that helps an individual keep track of all financial transactions.

Checking account
A type of bank account used for daily transactions.

Checks
A written document that tells a bank to pay for something from a user's bank account.

Community
A group of people who live in the same area or who have a common interest.

Complements
Goods that are used together.

Demand
A consumer's ability and willingness to buy goods and services.

Deposit
A certain amount of money put into a bank account.

Deposit Ticket
A receipt that a depositor (the person who puts money into the bank) receives when money is deposited.

Economy
A system of producing and selling goods and services of value.

Endorse Signature
The signature on the back of a check.

Free Enterprise
An economy where the goods and services sold, and the prices of goods and services are decided by the forces of supply and demand.

Goods
Physical objects that satisfy the wants of buyers.

Loan
An amount of money that is lent to a certain person or organization under an agreement that the money will be paid back in the future.

Management
The practice of supervising a project or people.

Market Economy
An economy where goods and services are privately owned and a profit incentive exists.

Merchandise
Goods that can be bought by consumers and sold by producers.

Net deposit
The total deposits (money put into the bank account) minus the total withdrawals (money taken out of the bank account) that were made using a certain method of payment.

Nonprofit
An organization that exists to serve people, rather than to make money.

Operating Costs
The costs that a business encounters on a daily basis.

Opportunity Cost
The value lost from the second best alternative that could have been chosen.

Philanthropy
Actions that help create a better society (e.g. donating to a nonprofit, volunteering for a charity, donating toys to a toy drive).

Profit
The money that a (for-profit) business makes. Profit = total revenue - total expenses.

Promissory note
A document that is signed by someone promising to pay a certain amount of money to another person or organization at the specified date or time.

Readiness
How prepared someone is for a certain job.

Receipt
A written document that confirms a transaction between two people or organizations.

Revenue
The income that a business receives from selling their goods or services. Revenue = price x quantity.

Savings account
A type of bank account that allows the money in the bank account to earn interest.

Scarcity
The idea that all valued resources are limited.

Sell
The act of giving something away in exchange for payment.

Services
Intangible actions that satisfy the wants of buyers.

Skill
The ability to do something well.

Substitutes
Goods that could be used instead of another good.

Supply
The amount of a good or service that producers are willing and able to sell at set prices.

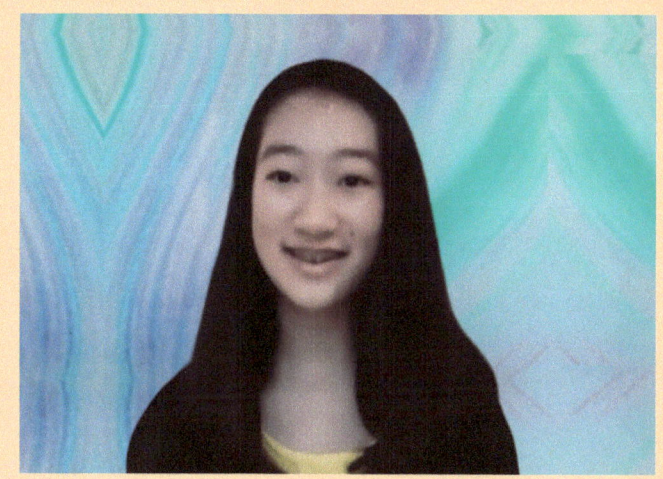

About the authors

Janet Liu & Melinda Liu both have a strong passion for economics. They are the founders of the 501(c)(3) nonprofit Sunrizon Economics, creators of the Wonderland Economics YouTube channel and the MyEconda e-learning platform, and the authors of *Economics for Tweens; A True Book: Making and Saving Money; and Making and Saving Money: Jobs, Taxes, Inflation... And Much More!*

They hope to share their love for economics with more students, helping them develop their understanding of economics from a young age.

Though they initially wrote this book in high school, Janet and Melinda are now studying Computer Science and Economics at MIT.

ADDITIONAL RESOURCES

Wonderland Economics Youtube Channel

 The videos on our Wonderland Economics YouTube channel accompany many of the concepts found in this book! Through fun and interactive videos, Orpple the monkey teaches fundamental economics concepts.

Sunrizon Economics, 501(c)(3) nonprofit

 Visit the Sunrizon Economics Website and subscribe to the mailing list if you are interested in getting economics competition opportunities and resources for K-12 students!

Economics for tweens—another book in this series!

 Check out our book *Economics for Tweens* to learn some slightly more advanced economics topics such as marginal analysis, production possibilities, and the types of business organizations!